DO NOT SEND ME OUT AMONG STRANGERS

Joshua Segun-Lean is a Nigerian writer, essayist, and photographer. His work has appeared in *The Brooklyn Rail*, *Jupiter Magazine*, and *Contemporary And*.

Do Not Send Me Out Among Strangers

JOSHUA SEGUN-LEAN

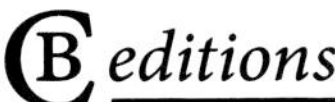

First published in Great Britain in 2024
by CB editions
146 Percy Road London W12 9QL
www.cbeditions.com

Printed in England by SRP Ltd, Exeter, Devon

ISBN 978-1-909585-56-0

Somewhere, for the sake of his children, a man
writes what he has seen

Somewhere, for the sake of his children, a man
will not write what he has seen

— Anne Michaels, *Fugitive Pieces*

It will take no forms but twisted forms

— Louise Glück, 'Elms'

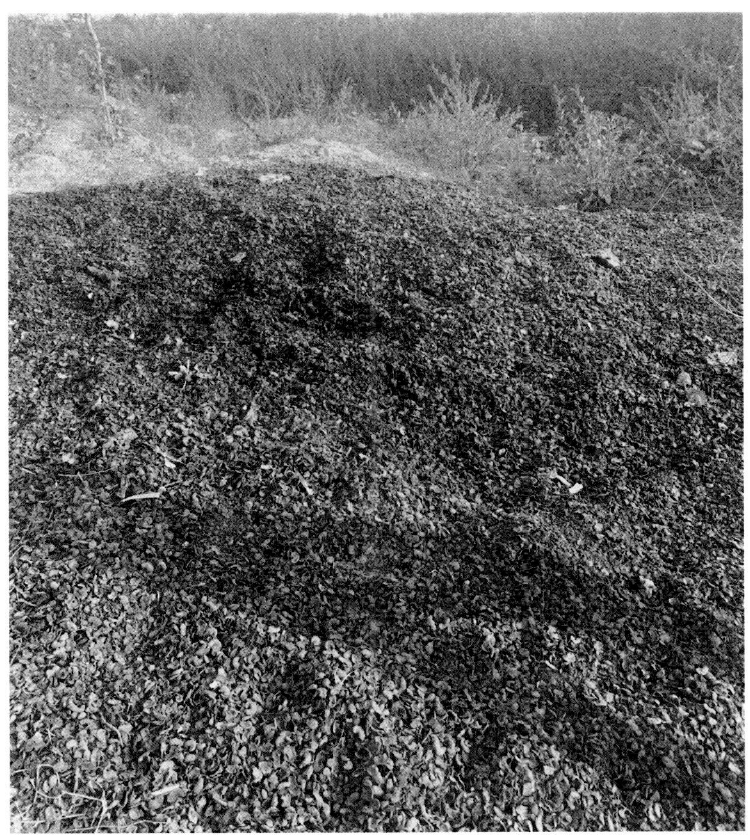

Field Notes #1, 8:14

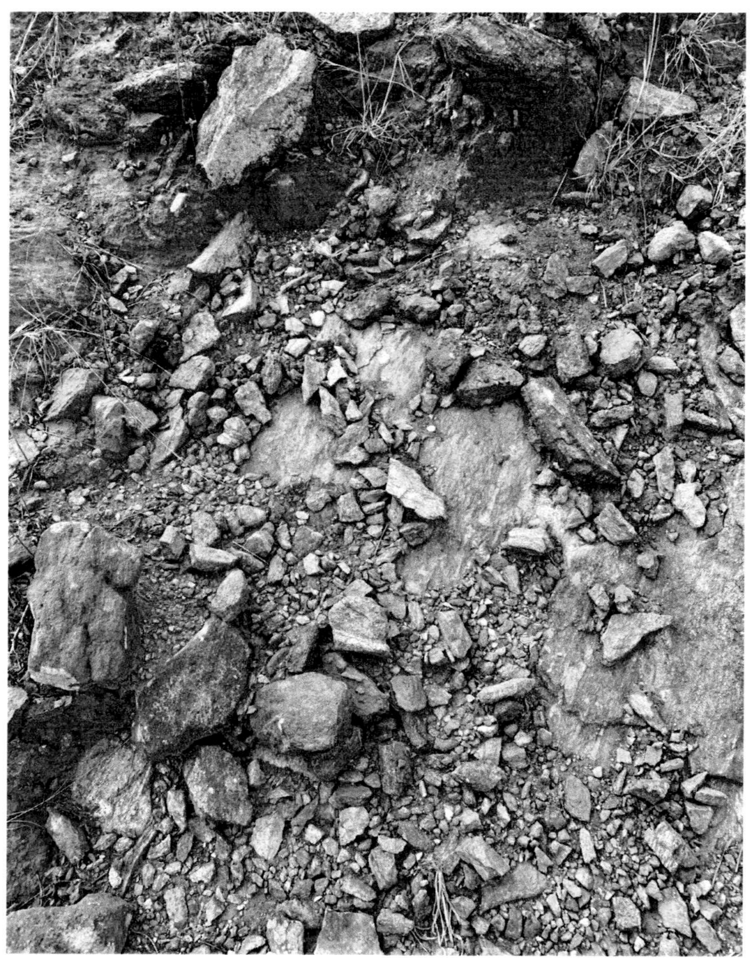

Field Notes #2, 8:57

'Yesterday, watching from the car window, I saw birds in perfect flight.' A sharp, clean sentence, and thus a promising beginning. Yet I have spent the last 6 hours attempting to revise it. After typing it out the first time it occurred to me that I have no reference for what imperfection in birds might look like. On what basis, then, could I have made this judgement? I don't know. It should not come to me so easily and yet it does. Imagining myself in the scale of a bird's life, in the altitudes of angels and lightning, the notion of perfection, the very word in my mind, feels immediately silly and shameful, like a sound released involuntarily from the body. So, we will put it away for now. I will try to describe, instead, what I saw: three rows of six, diving within and around a gradually expanding convex of air. They were like this, wing to wing, for several minutes and suddenly, as if responding to some urgent call, swung into a descending current and took off.

Only after I could no longer feel the echoes of wingbeat in my feet did I become conscious of myself and of the possibility of having been watched. I felt a jolt of fear. And then embarrassment. Why should this frighten me? But why shouldn't it? The fear of being caught looking, of being found in a state of engrossment seems not dissimilar from the fear of being caught naked but no one I have tried to explain it to understands. During the long bus rides of my childhood which I was forced to pass reading, I would often look up from my book to scan the faces of other passengers certain that I was the subject of quiet mockery. I believed once that I would outgrow it but with each decade I survive – even as the matters about which I should be more concerned grow in complexity and leave less room for squeamishness – I feel with increasing intensity the terror of revealing to strangers the existence of an inner life.

Anyway, the birds left and I stood there, and of course there was no one else around. It is still lockdown. Everyone is wherever everyone is when they are not in the streets. I came out to escape the familiarity of the house. It would be more bearable if I did not find everything exactly as I remembered it.

I am able to sleep after two hours of frenzied redecorating. I even moved the bed.

Now the trees, and not the neighboring house, are the first thing I see in the morning. My agent, John, asks if I have been writing. I lie and say no. Are you wearing your mask? All the time. How's the leg? Fine. A pause. Have you done it? No, not yet. Call me when you do. Okay. He is the latest to ask if I've 'done it' yet. A phrase everyone has adopted in reference to my father's ashes. I say that I am trying to find the right place. I don't think they believe me. Just as well. I don't know that I believe me.

Rereading my first entry. I understand now that the word 'perfect' is how we sometimes say 'This is beautiful. I don't think I will ever see this again' even though it is probable that we will. I hoped I could write about my father without writing about my shame. A failure. How to proceed? If to proceed?

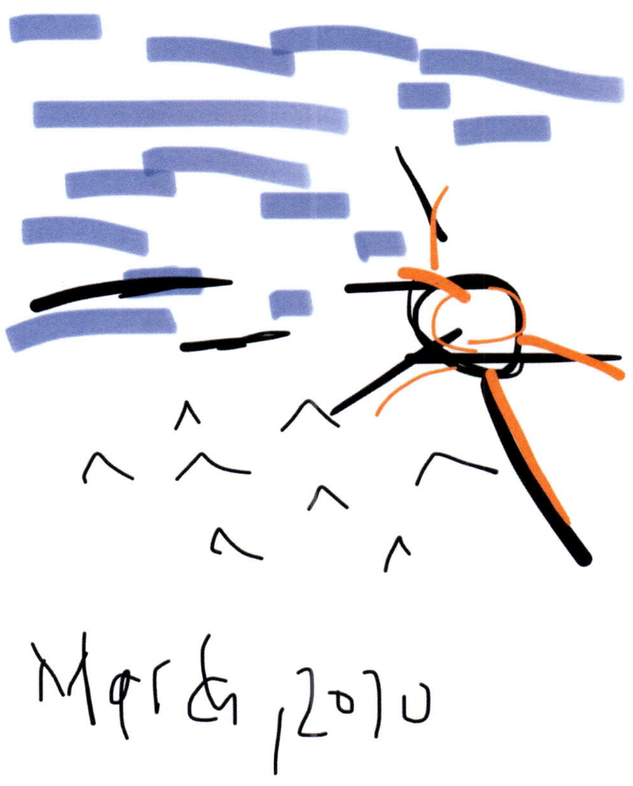

Sunny Day Out Quick Sketch.

Shopping: eggs, sardines, toilet rolls, lettuce, milk

Mortuary treatments, then, represent a nexus of the individual being buried and their social role in life as well as those doing the burying. Burial is a combination of what the deceased requested be done with their remains after death (if such a request was made), the interpretation and feelings about the deceased by the people doing the burying and their adherence to social norms, and the overarching social customs that guide and dictate how and why a certain burial type is employed.

– *The Odd, the Unusual, and the Strange: Bioarchaeological Interpretations of the Human Past: Local, Regional, and Global Perspectives.* Edited by Tracy K. Betsinger, Amy B. Scott and Anastasia Tsaliki.

First request: fire.

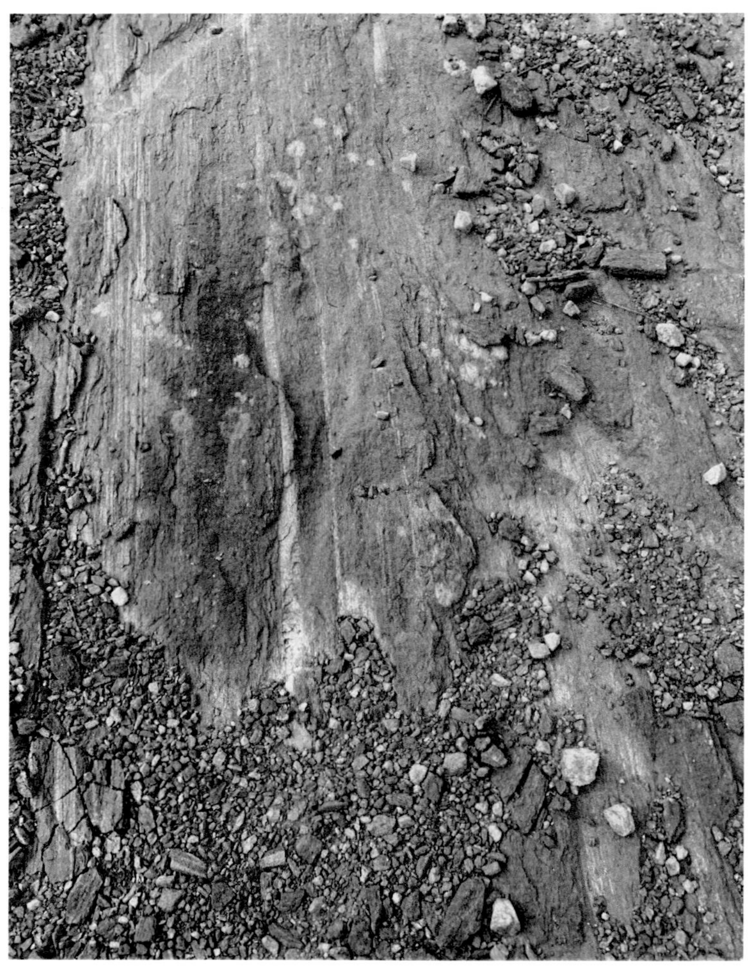

Field Notes #3, 7:10

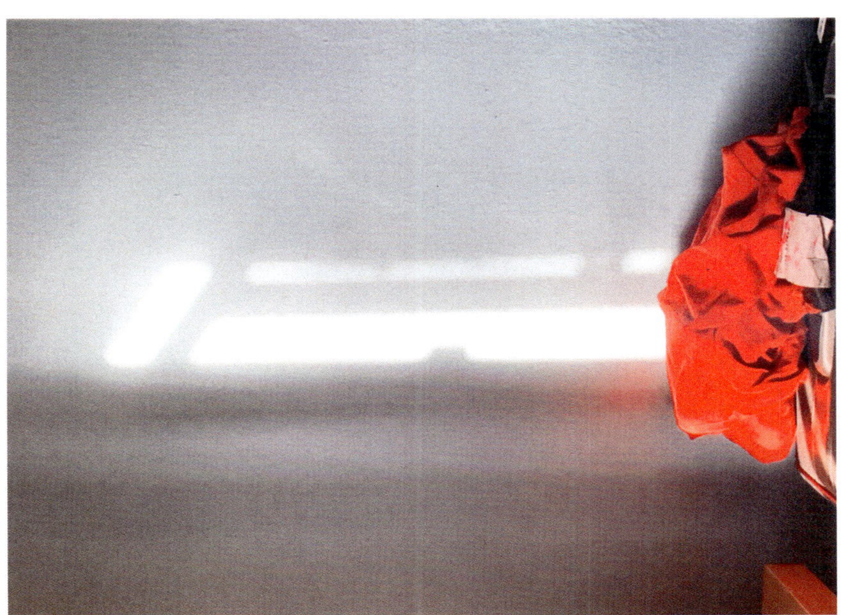

Interior #1, 8:30

Is this the color in certain Hopper paintings?

Perhaps it is too obvious to think of Hopper in times like this.

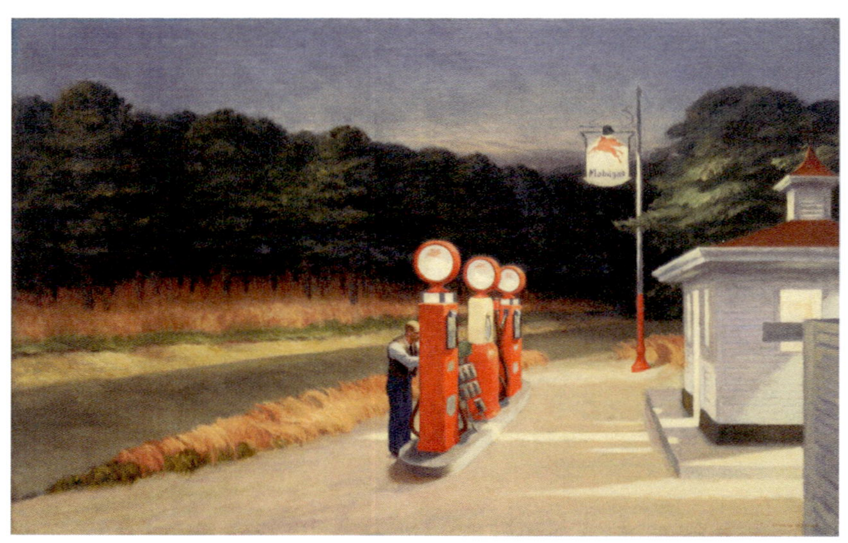

Edward Hopper, *Gas*, 1940

Here?

Having never tried journaling until now, I can't say if I'm doing a good job. Of all the activities people recommend for 'staying positive' through the pandemic, journaling seemed the most obvious choice for me. Though I have set no grand expectations for myself, I'm afraid I will be unable to keep from filling each page, eventually, with minutiae. With the flatness of time as it passes here. An instinct, I think, from an earlier, truncated life in the sciences. Or perhaps like the voice in Sans Solei, 'I have been around the world several times, and now only banality still interests me.'

I am not that far gone, I don't think.

Today, I overheard Abel whistle as he watered the plants. It was a song I'd never heard before. Immediately I reached for this book, hoping I might put down the lyrics. But I thought better of it and lay back down until he stopped. When I return later, covered head to toe in dust, he hardly seems to notice and asks no questions. Same as the last time and the time before. I am surprised by my disappointment. I usually admire such discretion in people. But I want him to ask. I want to explain what I'm looking for. So far, I have offered him nothing more of myself than is necessary to cohabit peaceably, and yet I would not hesitate, should he ask, to divulge every last detail of the past few months. Though I experience this impulse in myself as a weakness, I am often moved by it in others. It is no surprise that among the Sacraments of Penance and Reconciliation in the Catholic tradition in which I was raised, the confession alone still interests me. Even the most reticent of us harbours a deep and painful wish to be exposed. A childish desire to be found out.

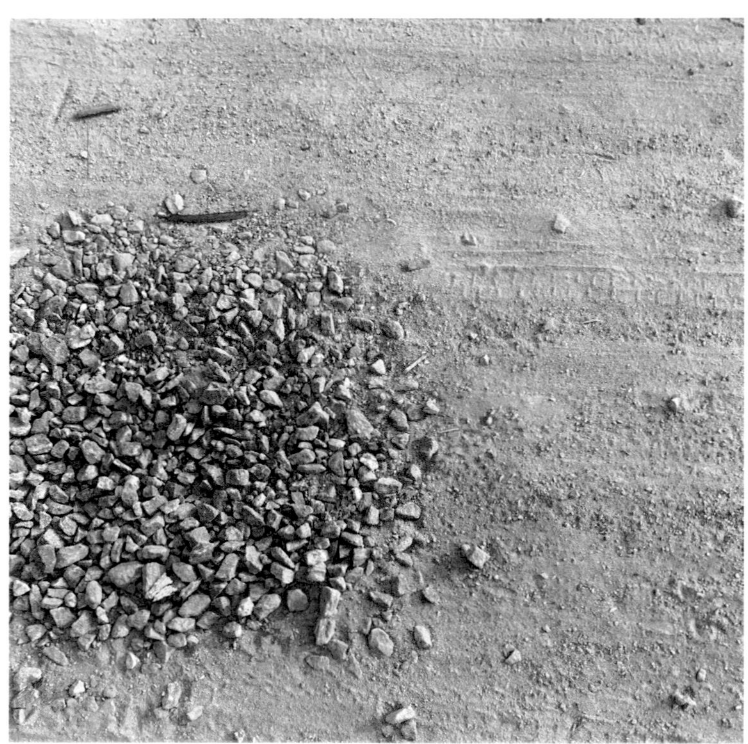

Field Notes #4, 9:14

I am trying to follow the news. I am afraid of following the news.
I am afraid it will follow me back here.

5 friends so far have caught the virus. No one wants to tell me
how bad it is because they think I have problems enough. Can't
they see that I am always worrying, anyway? I send my neighbor
back home some of the things I've been making. You're drawing
again? A little. Mostly doodles, sketches. Nothing much, really.
How long will you be there for? I don't know. I planned to stay
only a few days but, you know. I miss you and the kids. They must
be driving you crazy. I've been going on hikes. They'd like it here.
You'll be careful? I will. I'm sorry again about your father. It's
okay.

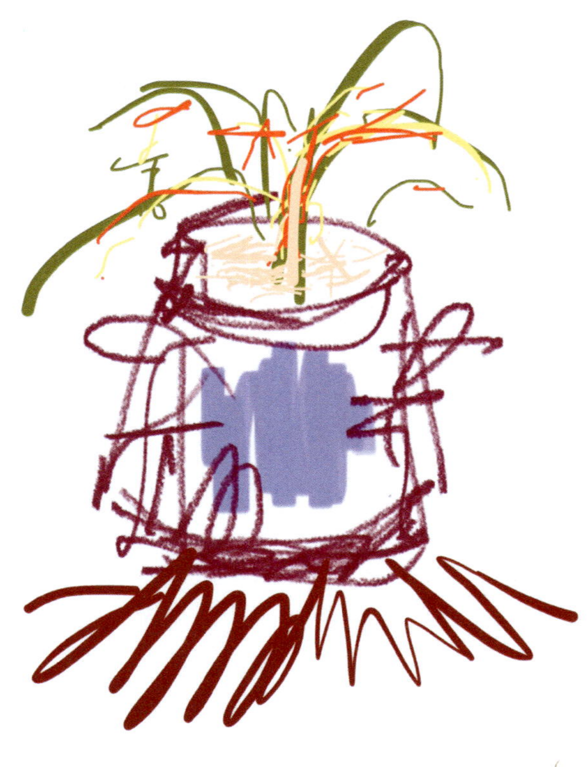

Vase Study

Sometimes I have nothing to say.

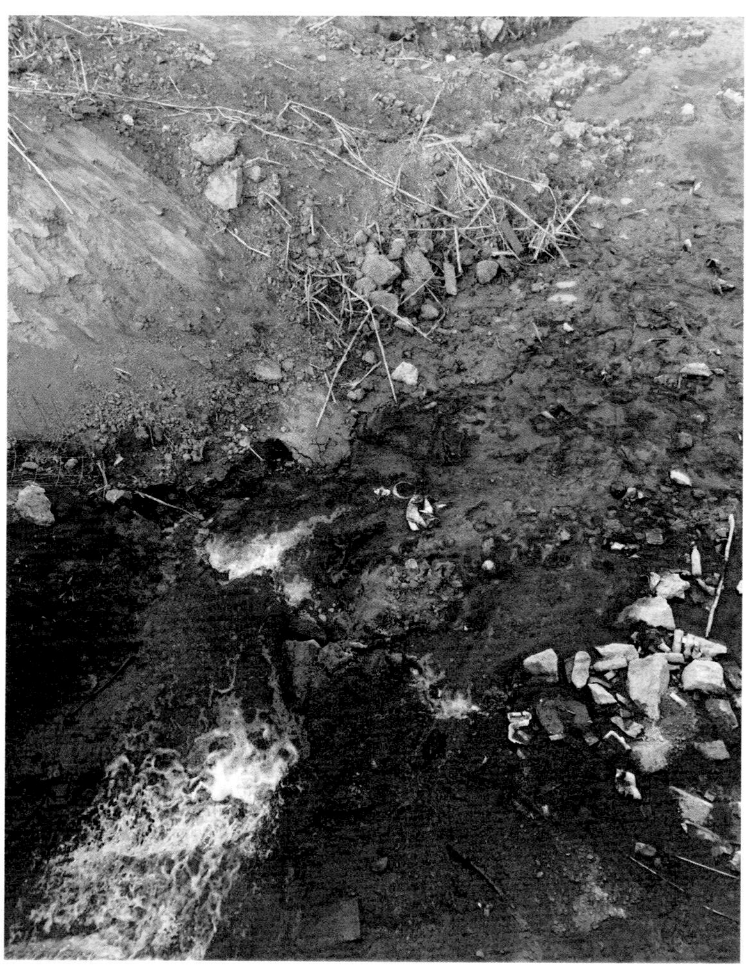

Field Notes #5, 10:44

Take, for instance, the Varna Burials in Bulgaria (*c.*4500 BC).
About 25 percent of the graves at this site are empty, lacking
the remains of the body. Nitra, in Slovakia, is another case that
also contains numerous empty graves. Do these 'centotaphs'
represent individuals that thave died far away, or perhaps
at sea, leaving no body to be buried? Or do these empty
'graves' correspond to individuals that have died an 'unnatural'
death, or are they perhaps even statements for the socially,
but not yet phyiscally dead?

Can we extend the definition of a grave to also include a
final resting place for artefacts? [. . .] The question is all about
representation rather than symbolism. Ginsburg (2002:72)
describes the case of a dead ruler that was buring twice at
two different locations. One grave contains the body, while
the other holds a material representation of the ruler. The
interesting aspect of this case is that it was the grave with the
representation that was considered the 'real' one.

The Materiality of Death: Bodies, Burials, Beiefs.
Edited by Fredrik Fahlander and Terje Oestigaard.

As I wasn't there, I cannot say what state my father was in when
he asked that I be the one to scatter his remains. I don't know
if he meant it as punishment or as some strange attempt at
reconciliation. He could not be sure that I would accept, could he?
Who would be here in my place if I had not?

It was not a body I had known well. I rarely saw him without
clothes as a child. And what parts went uncovered never
possessed individual significance. I could not isolate them. He
moved as one heavy thing. Standing close to him was to see
both the fact of his body and the negative space around it, as
with especially large statues or buildings. It was easier to see and
remember the shape of his body than the body itself.

Now there is only the shape, stark in my mind like a hole through
a wall.

Today I read that all the hospitals are full.

When I started going on these hikes, I decided to take my camera
along on a whim. I'm glad I did. I sent all the photos in the 'Field
Notes' folder to Rachel, a former student. She thinks they're
'bleak' but 'striking' and asks if I'm being careful. You know,
about your leg. I say I know. After the call, I prepare to set out
again.

I'm working on a theory that landscapes from which people have
been forced to move for whatever reason evoke a different kind of
desolation from those which have never known human presence.
Desolation from the Latin *desolatus* – abandoned. I felt this often
as a child waking up to find that everyone had gone to Mass.
Perfumes and powders still strong in the air, half-empty mugs
in the sink, items of clothing which, decided against at the last
minute, were flung on whatever surface was closest. My mind, still
righting itself from sleep, found such scenes immensely dramatic.
Ghostlike. I wandered through the house as a stranger would, in
slow, halting steps, even though every aspect of it was instantly
familiar to me. Neither the knowledge that the house would be
full again in a few hours nor my ever-present craving for moments
of solitude could pierce the confusion and alienation I felt in
those few moments.

Will stay in bed today.

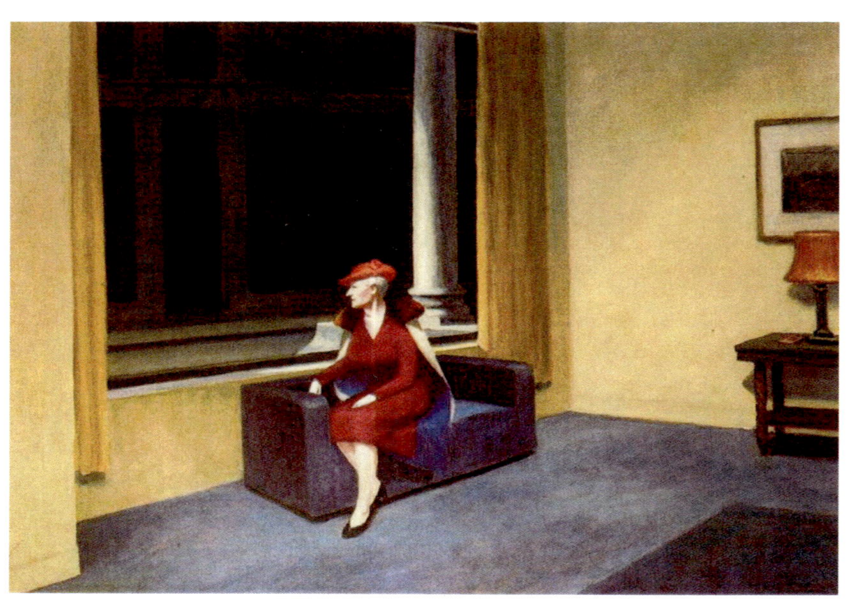

Edward Hopper, *Hotel Window*, 1955

Or here?

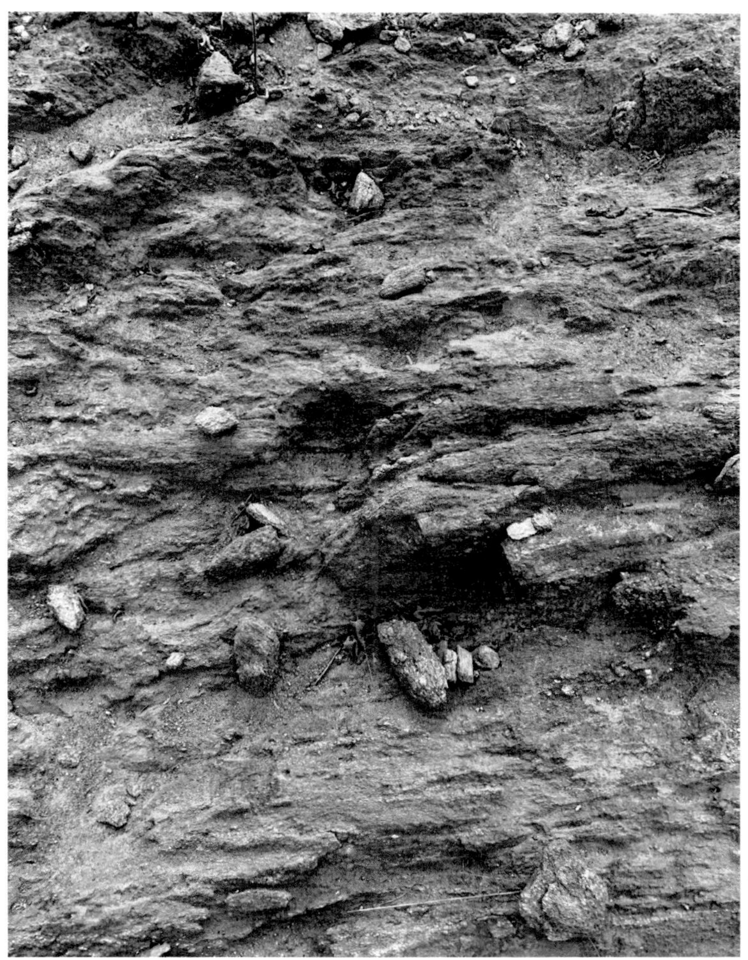

Field Notes #6, 8:32

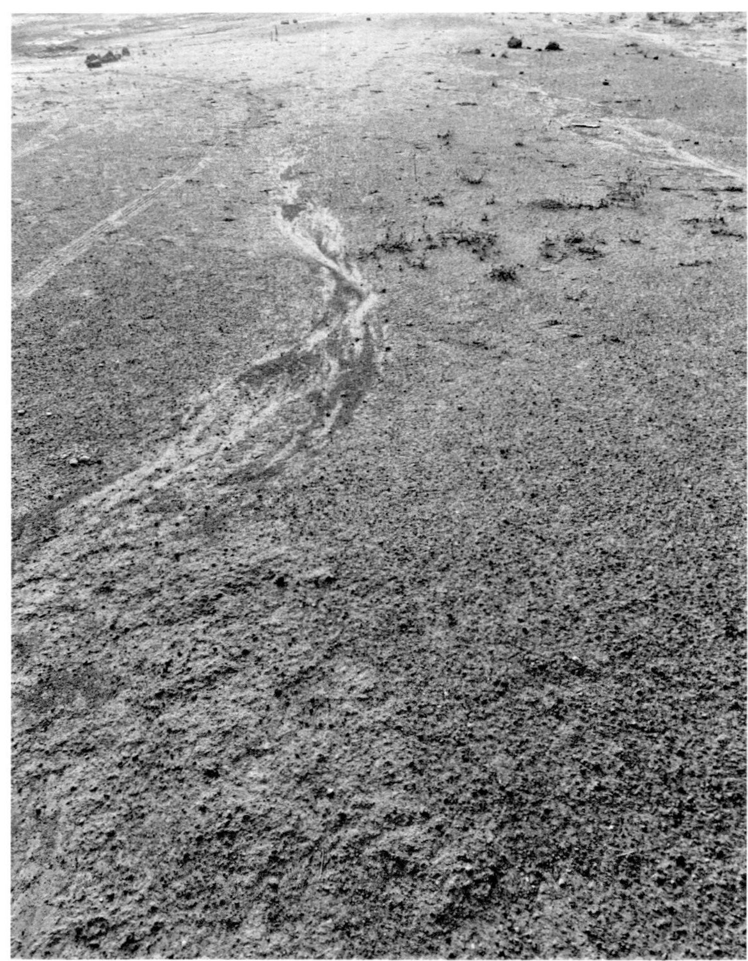

Field Notes #7, 11:09

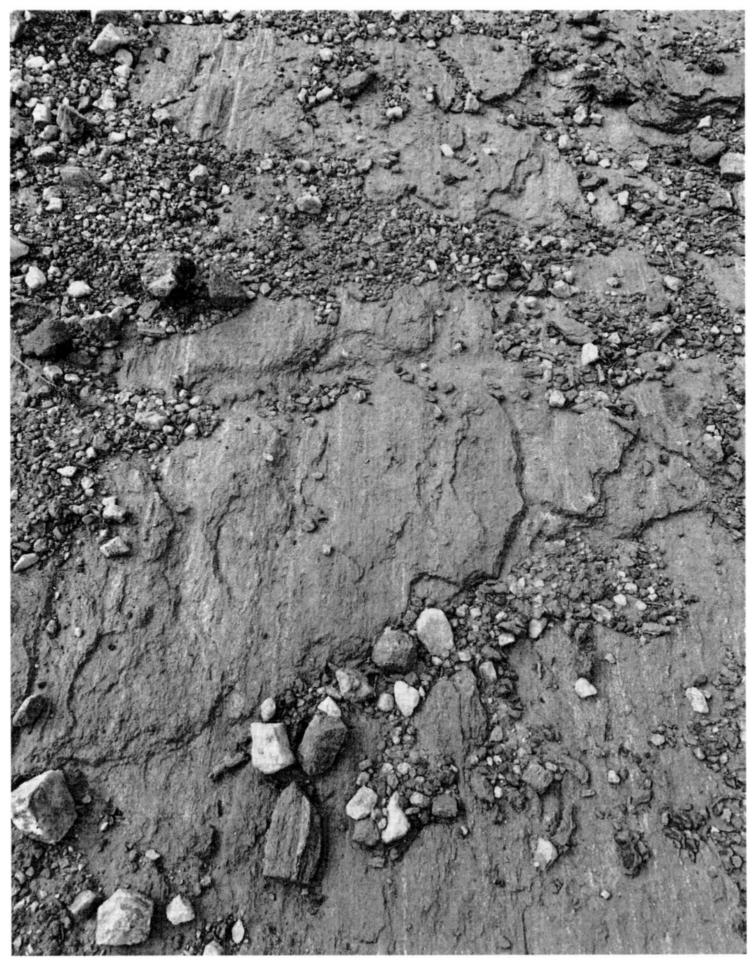

Field Notes #8, 7:23

Carrying the camera and urn for long hours has begun to take a toll but I manage alright. Some days, I go thrice, morning, after lunch, and just before sunset. On FaceTime, I tell John I think I have found the place and that I've been writing. Not sure yet but I think the 'pandemic journal' might be an interesting evolution of an idea we'd spoken about before. I'll send what I have soon.

In the dream I keep having, my father hikes with me. Our legs strain for purchase on the ground but make no sound. The quiet is so complete it feels like the end of something.

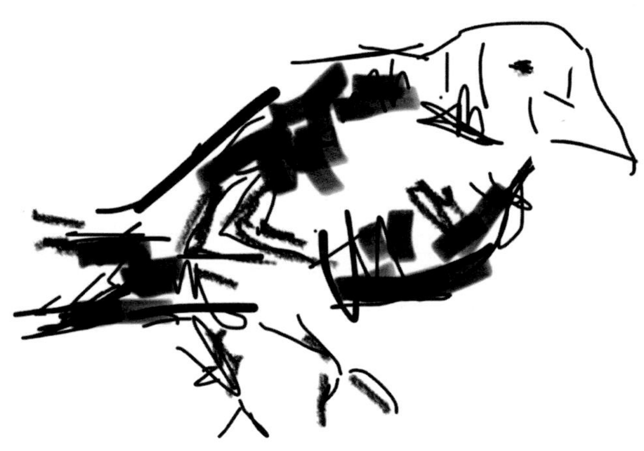

Bird Study #1

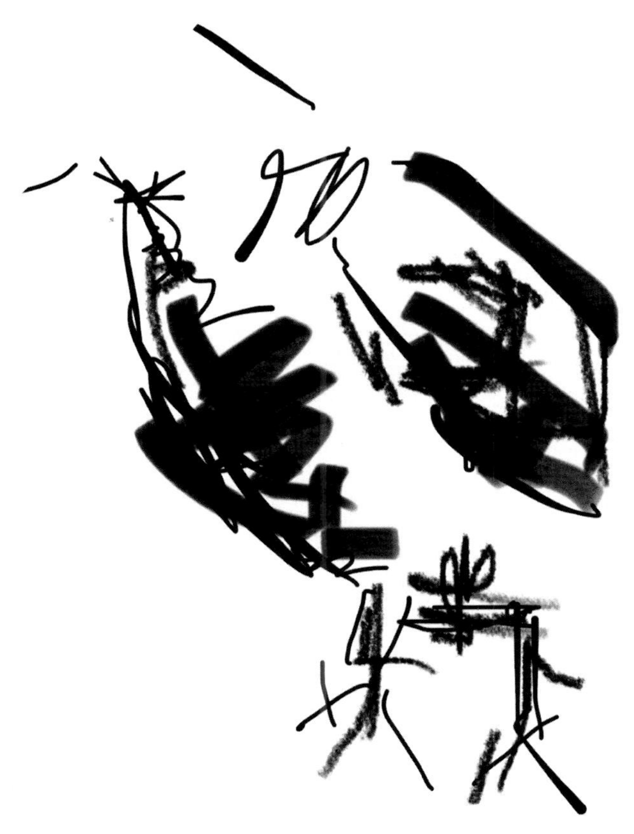

Bird Study #2

Fourthly, at times of death on Crusade in non-Christian
countries, the bodies of the elite were sometimes burned and
the hearts embalmed so that Christian remians were portable
and brought home. This division of body parts after death
was forbidden by Pope Boniface VII in 1299. More commonly,
at times of plague, the claims of public health and survival
permitted bodies of the plague dead to be burned. Burning
the dead was for emergencies.

Dust to Ashes: Cremation and the British Way of Death
by Peter C. Jupp.

For no reason, I tell Abel this morning that I'll turn 42 in 2 weeks. He asks if we should expect visitors, my wife and children perhaps, so he can pick up more things at the market. I am pleased by his interest. I say no, you know how everything is. For no reason, after a moment, I tell him I cannot have children. I ask if he has any. A boy and a girl. He shows me their faces on his screensaver. They have his face.

Until now, I have carried this knowledge, the very memory of being told what the accident had done to me, in a sealed valve in my mind. Not because I haven't wished to remember it but because I have wanted to keep it separate from other memories, under special conditions which might resist the withering of time. I had preserved it with such diligence that with every recollection, the details seem sharper, higher in resolution. I can smell the gauze and the too-clean smell hospital floors always have. I know what's on the television and I can see the hairs on my father's head where the hairline was yet to recede.

After the doctor leaves, he looks up not at me but at some point over the bed, where the room's yellow paint had begun to chip, and says, 'How will you live a man's life?'

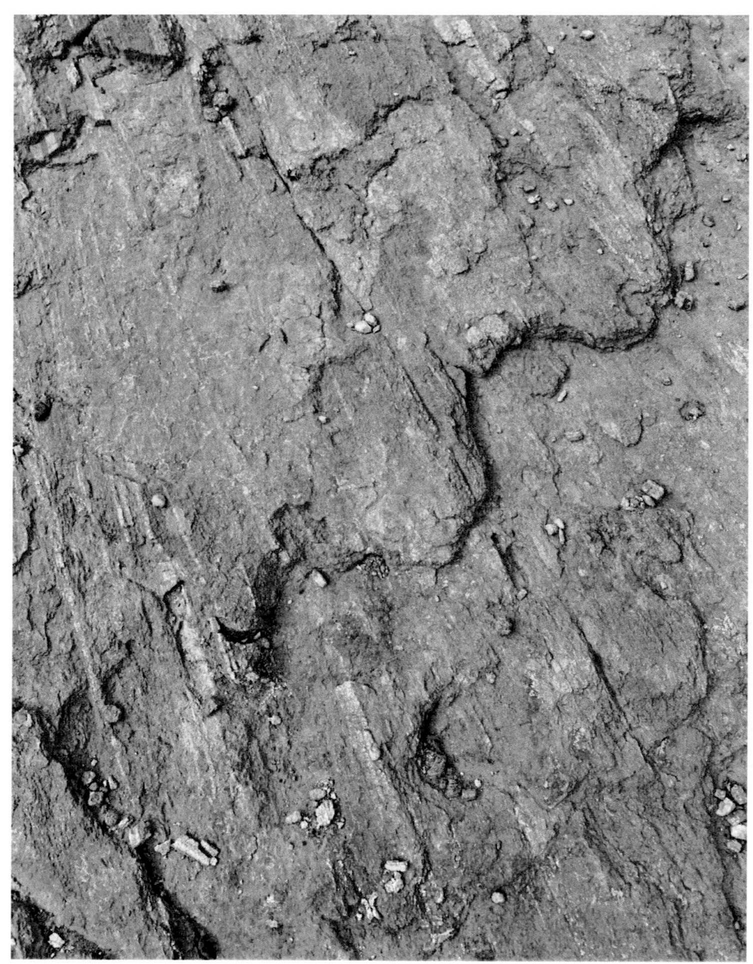

Field Notes #9, 11:33

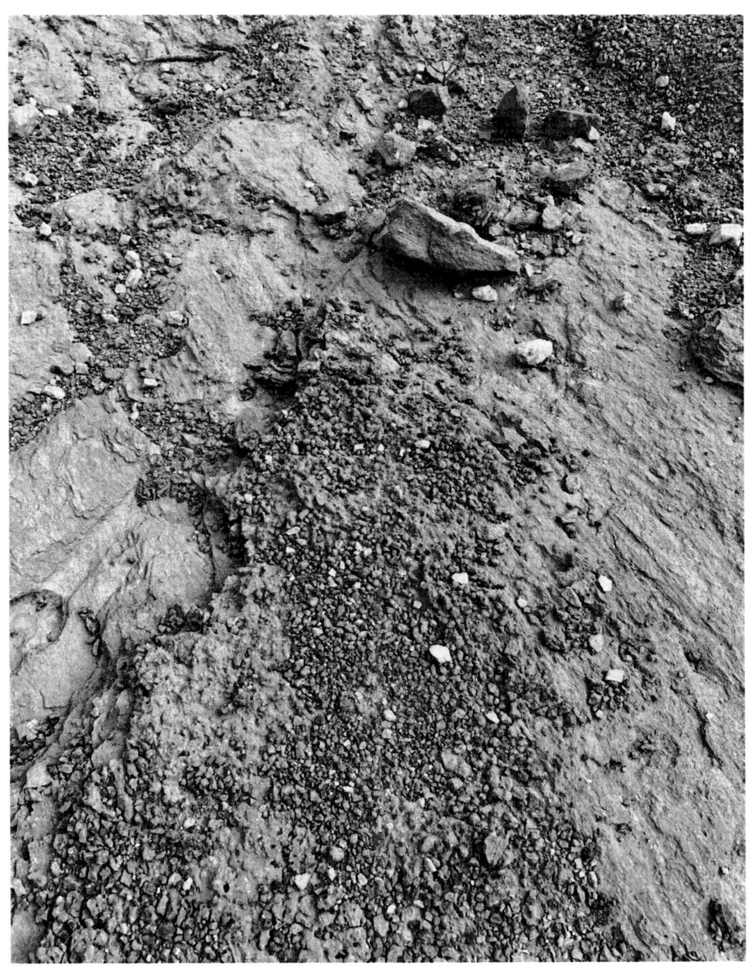

Field Notes #10, 14:00

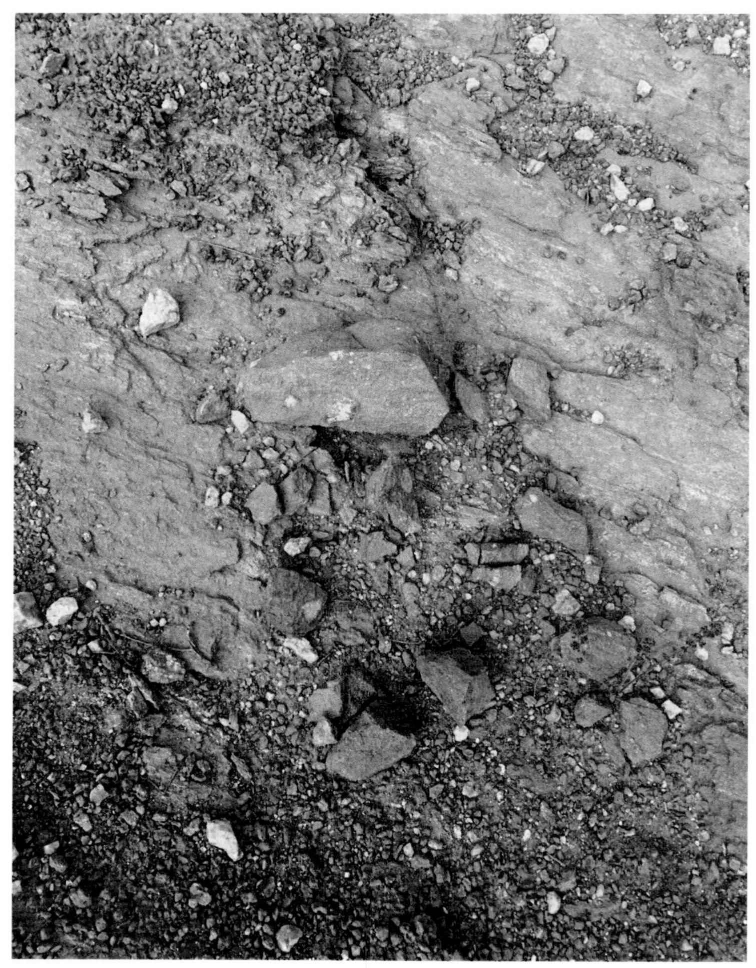

Field Notes #11, 8:12

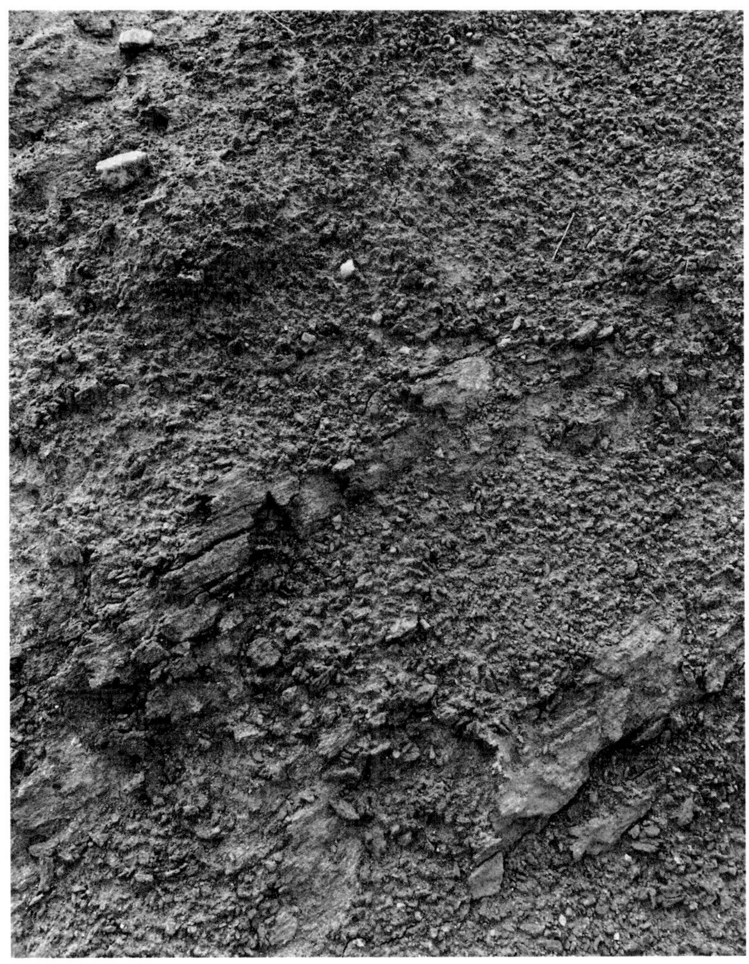

Field Notes #12, 17:26

Fix bathroom door downstairs.
Throw away old newspapers in the library.
Change the curtains with Abel.

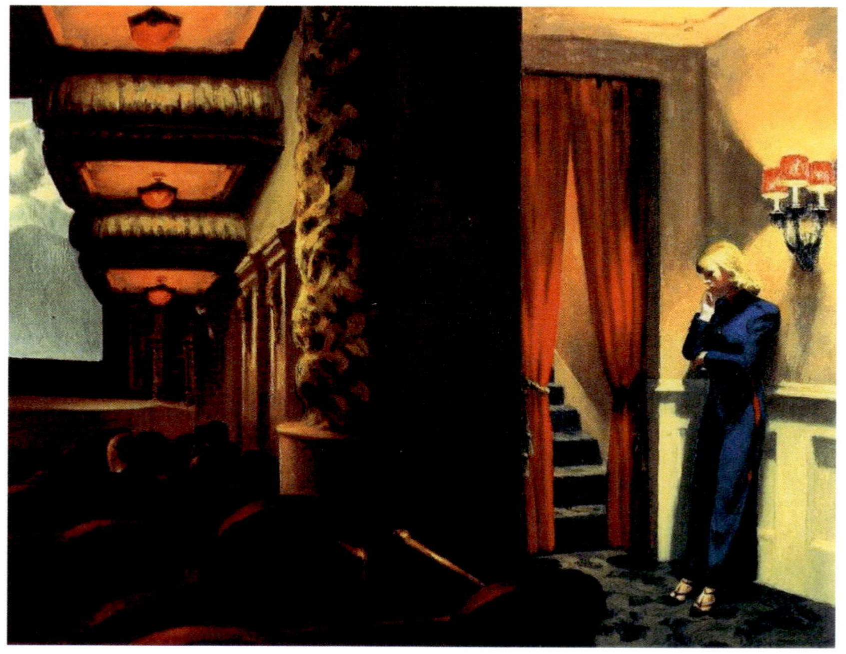

Edward Hopper, *New York Movie*, 1939

Here?

Joseph Stanton has a poem about this painting. I will find it.

8 friends now in critical condition. I can't find oat milk anywhere.

I don't know what I'm doing.

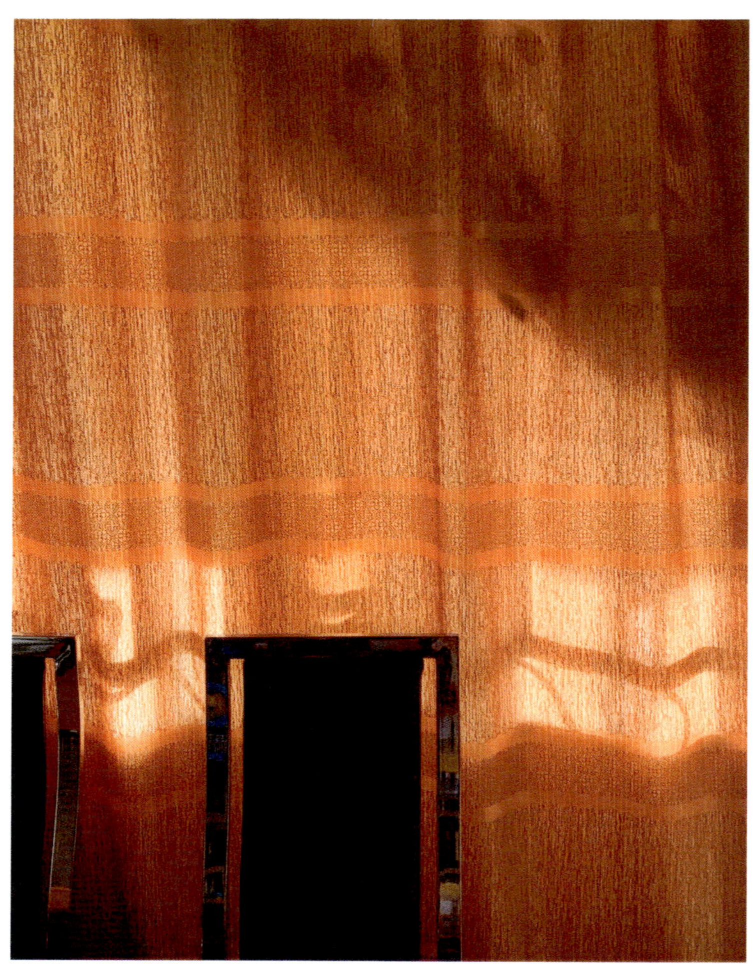

Interior #2, 16:23

Thus we arrive at the death instinct: the instinct to return to
the inanimate state. Freud speaks of the origin of conscious
life as a kind of response of the inanimate to some external
force and then, once coming into existence, of the desire to be
free from it again. Others had used similar ideas before him
and one of his biographers even suggested that Freud came
to use the novel phrase 'death-instinct' only a few weeks after
experiencing the death of his daughter Sophie.

Death, Ritual and Belief by Douglas Davis.

In my Theories of Grief class, I try to explain the essential disorientation experienced by the wounded mind, which is never settled between its need of specificity and its need of abstraction. When the force, the closeness of detail becomes unbearable, we require a swift withdrawal to that place where no meaning is consistent, fixed or entirely knowable. And when in this region of no borders the sufferer finds herself unmoored, she reaches for the strictest confine, inexorable dimension, for the miracle of the fact.

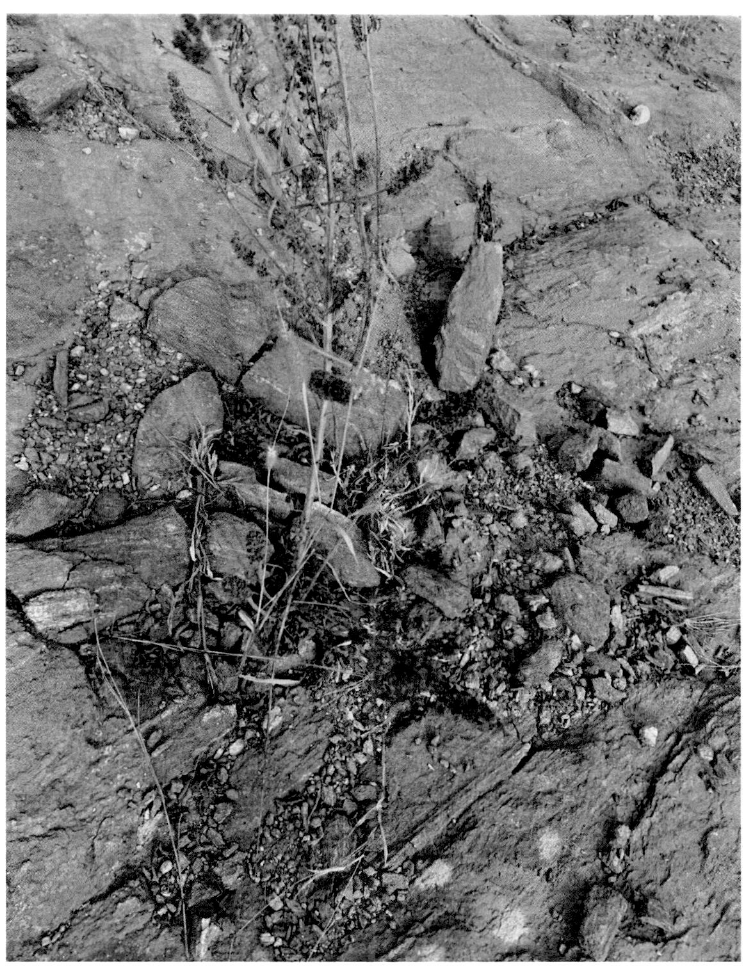

Field Notes #13, 12:34

I never meet anyone when I walk here but I always find fresh
footprints. Other signs of human activity, bits of rubbish scattered
by the wind. If you're here, why won't you let me see you?

Tell me where to let you go. I don't know what I'm doing.

Because it had taken nearly a whole day to find a way to bring me out of the car, my father had gotten to the hospital before I did, following a 5-hour flight, and already signed up as a donor. When I came to, I learned he was well known among the staff, having taken up odd tasks around the hospital. I had known him well enough to understand this as his own way of passing time. He hated nothing more than waiting for things to happen.

I am the son of a man whose patience with life was so short he refused even the possibility of decomposing.

I am the son who will bear no son.

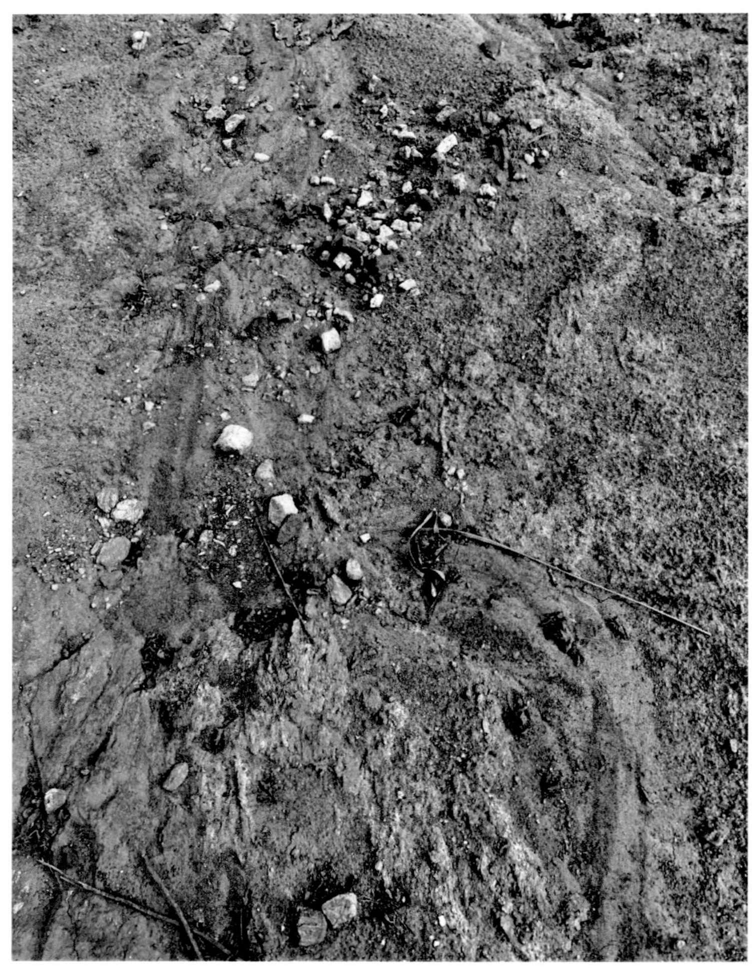

Field Notes #14, 13:06

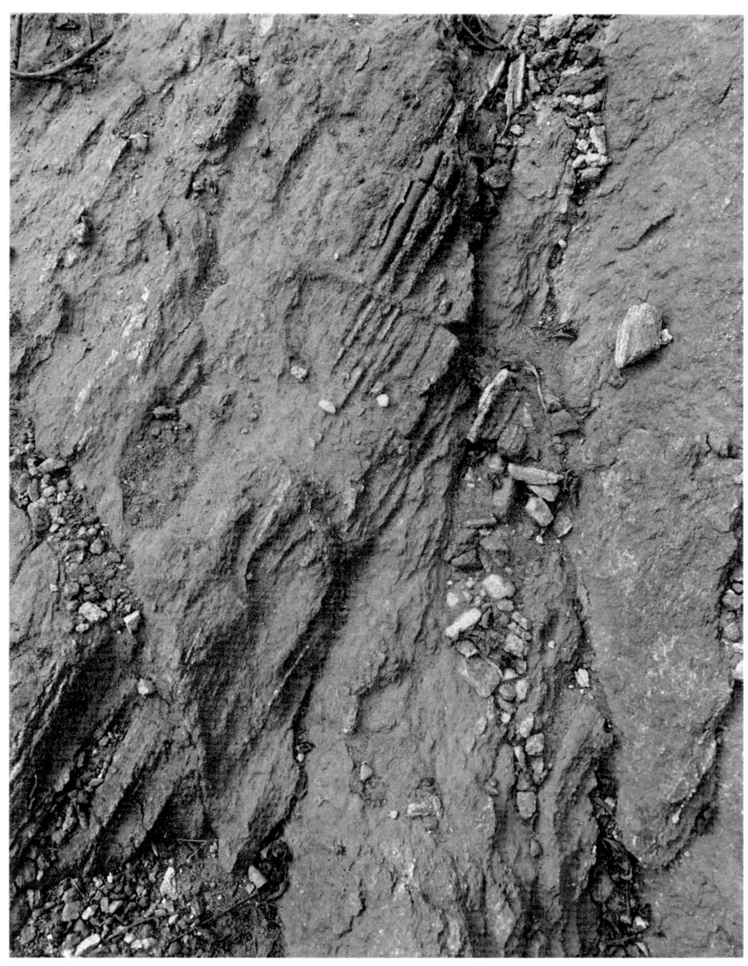

Field Notes #15, 7:47

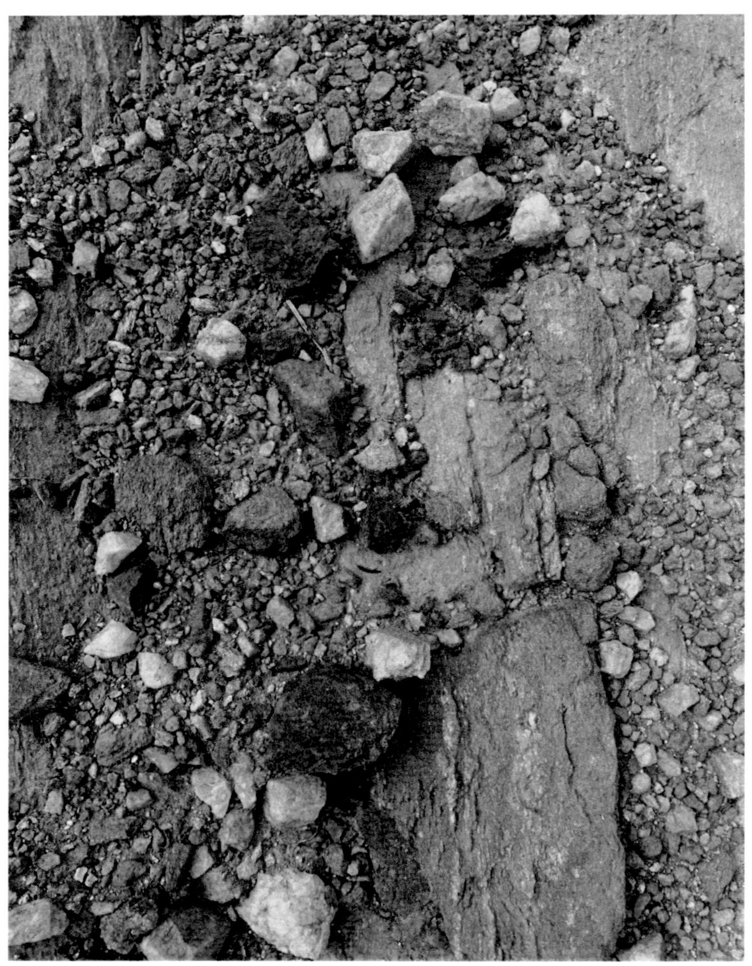

Field Notes #16, 9:56

I went farther today than I'd ever gone, almost at the very top
of the first hill where a rush of young plants had been growing,
still sated from the rainy months. As I turned in a bend, I sensed
sudden movement. I wasn't quick enough to see the insect itself
but I saw the leaf it must have perched on flutter. I watched until
it became still.

What the eye does not sustain in the instant is groped for in the
afterimage. The photoreceptor cells assailed, forever, against time.
And in the vacuum of the eye into which the image nearly enters,
a lingering which can only be described as the passing of light's
shadow.

        Here we are an accidental
fellowship, sheltering from the city's
obscure bereavements to face a screened,
        imaginary living,
as if it were a destination
we were moving toward.

From 'Edward Hopper's New York Movie' by Joseph Stanton.

I have just left the second Zoom funeral in three days. There is
nothing obscure about these bereavements.

Man's neotony, the long period of time he spends in the
process of learning, forging a new relationship between
young and old, above all between son and father, in which
the catastrophe of death became especially disturbing and
dangerous.

*Homo Necans: The Anthropology of Ancient Greek Sacrificial
Ritual and Myth* by Walter Burkert.

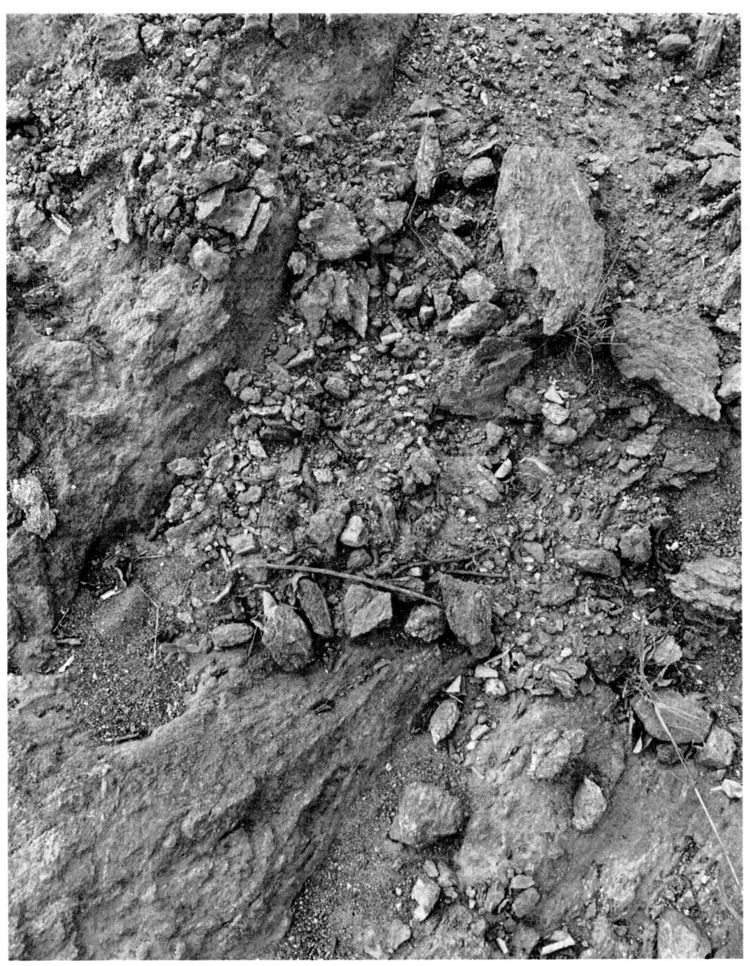

Field Notes #17, 15:18

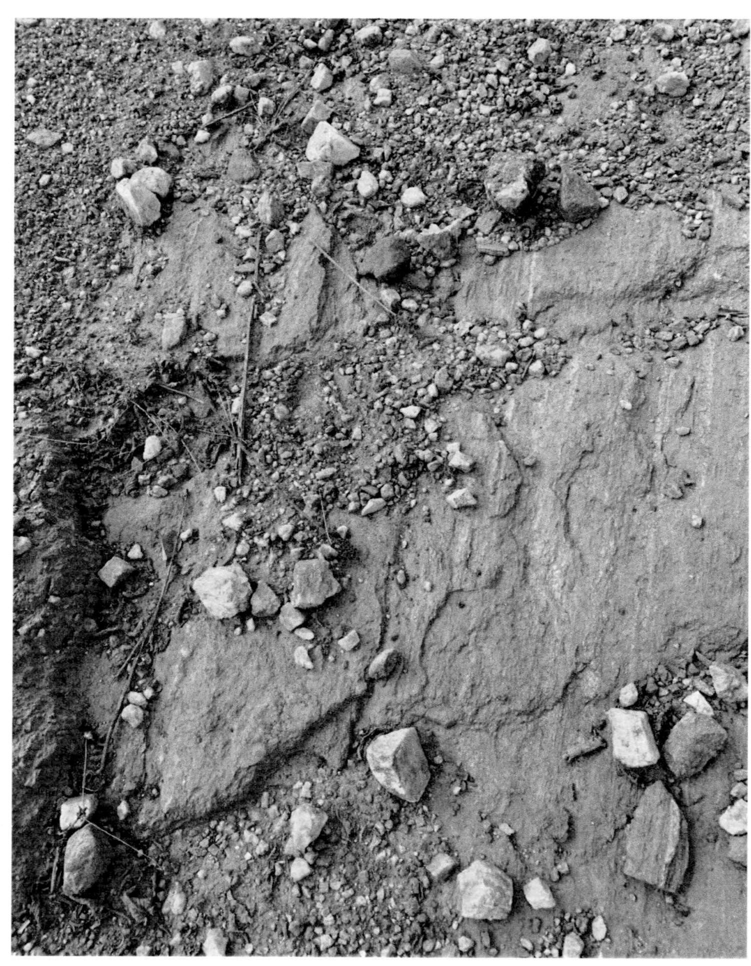

Field Notes #18, 9:18

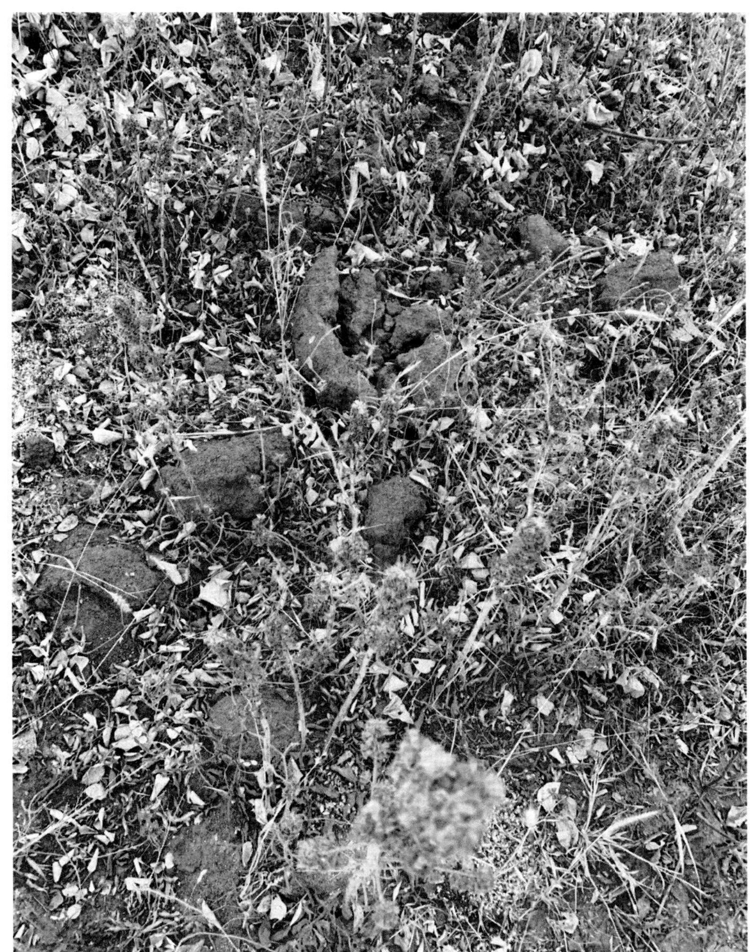

Field Notes #19, 7:45

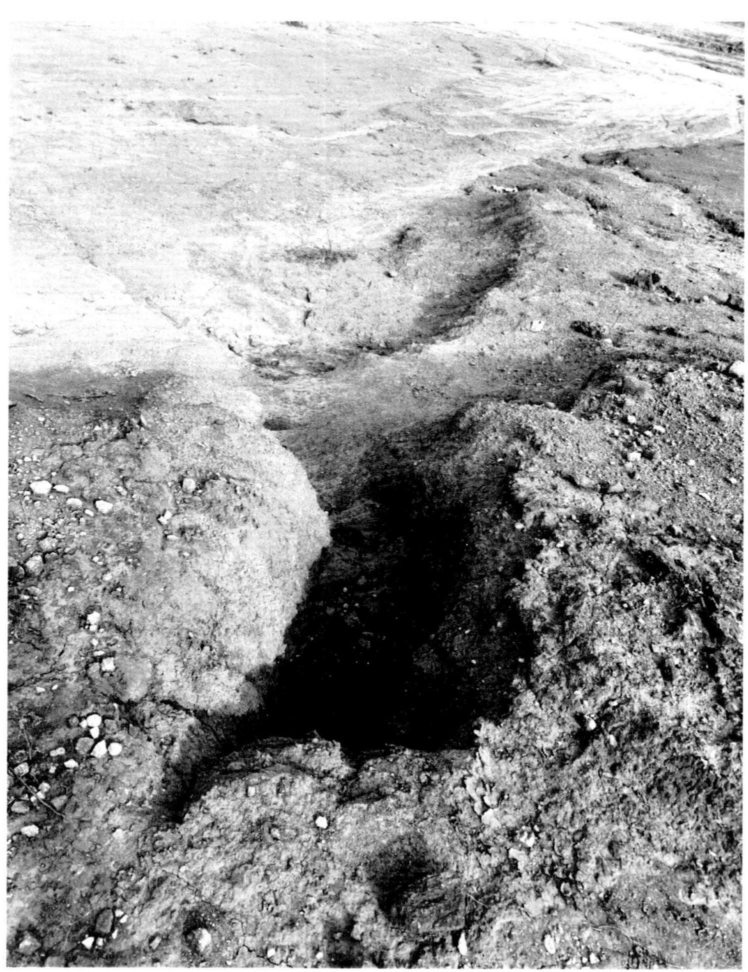

Field Notes #20: 11:17

The trees outside my window are lemon trees. I smell them in my sleep.

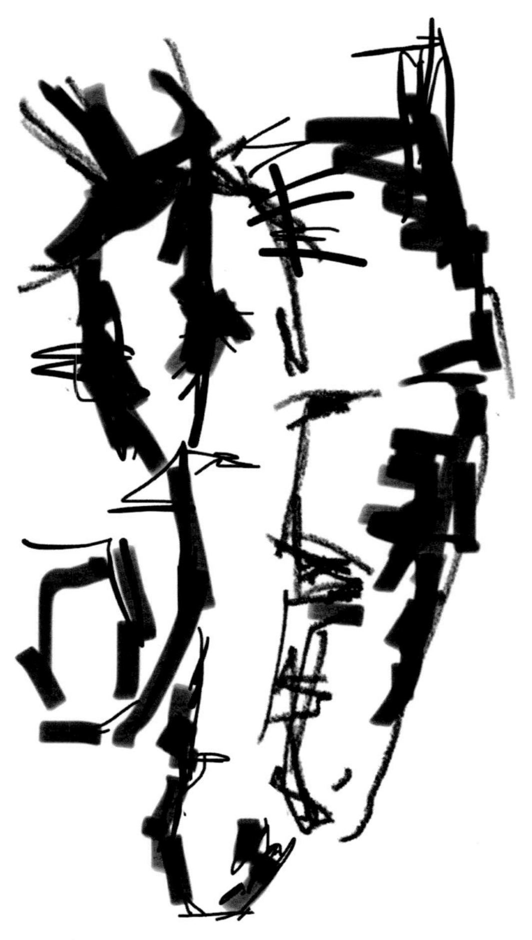

Fingers in ash study #1

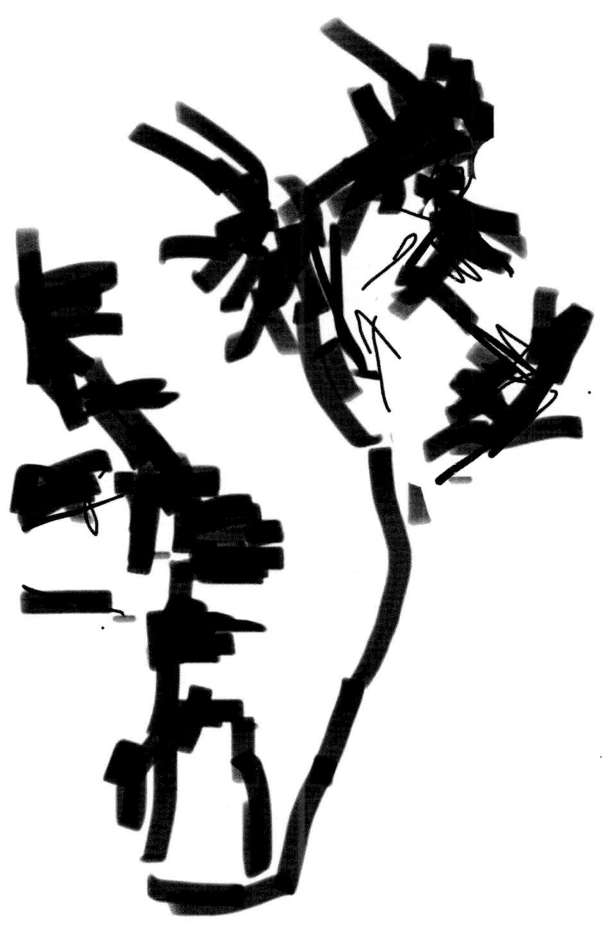

Fingers in ash study #2